LAST

7/11 0X

/ / / /

CR

D0772223

DOGS SET I

COCKER SPANIELS

Heidi Mathea
ABDO Publishing Company

visit us at
www.abdopublishing.com

Published by ABDO Publishing Company, 8000 West 78th Street, Edina, Minnesota 55439. Copyright © 2011 by Abdo Consulting Group, Inc. International copyrights reserved in all countries. No part of this book may be reproduced in any form without written permission from the publisher. The Checkerboard Library™ is a trademark and logo of ABDO Publishing Company.

Printed in the United States of America, North Mankato, Minnesota.
042010
092010

 PRINTED ON RECYCLED PAPER

Cover Photo: Corbis
Interior Photos: Corbis pp. 9, 10–11; Getty Images pp. 7, 11, 15, 16–17;
    Peter Arnold pp. 14, 19; Photolibrary pp. 5, 13, 21

Editor: BreAnn Rumsch
Art Direction & Cover Design: Neil Klinepier

Library of Congress Cataloging-in-Publication Data

Mathea, Heidi, 1979-
 Cocker spaniels / Heidi Mathea.
     p. cm. -- (Dogs)
 Includes index.
 ISBN 978-1-61613-404-4
 1. Cocker spaniels--Juvenile literature. I. Title.
 SF429.C55M28 2011
 636.752'4--dc22

                                    2010009923

CONTENTS

The Dog Family

Dogs have been living with humans for more than 12,000 years. Today, more than 400 **breeds** exist. All dogs belong to the family **Canidae**. This name comes from the Latin word *canis*, which means "dog."

Today's dogs descend from the gray wolf. Some dogs, such as the friendly cocker spaniel, look nothing like the wolf. But, dogs and wolves still share instincts.

The cocker spaniel is one of today's popular hunting breeds. This active dog is speedy and loves water. It is also an affectionate animal that serves as a perfect companion dog.

The cocker spaniel is the twenty-third most popular breed in the United States.

COCKER SPANIELS

Cocker spaniels are playful, loving dogs. This **breed**'s roots date back to at least the 1300s. Historians believe spaniels came from Spain. Humans bred them to be hunting dogs.

The smallest of the spaniel breeds is the cocker spaniel. This dog is named for its ability to hunt birds called woodcocks.

The **American Kennel Club** registered the cocker spaniel as a breed in 1878. Today, the cocker spaniel still loves to hunt. This active dog happily **flushes** and **retrieves** game. And it enjoys swimming. The cocker also makes a great family pet.

These happy dogs will gladly sit on your lap or go for a run.

WHAT THEY'RE LIKE

Cocker spaniels are beautiful dogs. Few people can resist their friendly manner. Many people forget cockers were first **bred** to be great all-around hunting dogs.

As hunters, cockers have a good sense of hearing. They can detect sounds that are too high-pitched for humans to hear. And, they can pick up sounds at great distances.

Cockers also have a keen sense of smell. They learn about their world by sniffing everything around them. These sporting dogs can remember thousands of scents! They even link certain smells with particular people, places, and other animals.

Like any good hunting breed, the cocker can keep up a fast pace for hours.

COAT AND COLOR

The cocker spaniel has a long, soft, silky coat. The coat can be flat or wavy. This cheerful dog has long hair on its ears, chest, belly, and legs. This gives the cocker a feathered look. Some cockers look like they are wearing long, fringed skirts on each leg!

Cockers come in a variety of colors. They can be solid black or black with tan markings. They can also be any solid color from light cream to dark red.

Some cockers have parti-color coats. These coats display two or more solid colors. A parti-color cocker may be black and white, red and white, or brown and white.

Cocker spaniels have dark brown eyes.

SIZE

The cocker spaniel is the smallest member of the sporting dog group. Cockers weigh 22 to 29 pounds (10 to 13 kg). Males stand 15 inches (38 cm) from the ground to their shoulders. Females are shorter at 14 inches (36 cm) high.

Straight, powerful legs support this active dog's compact body and broad chest. The cocker spaniel's head is rounded with a square, bold **muzzle**. This alert dog has slightly almond-shaped eyes. Its big eyebrows give it a sweet, intelligent expression.

Long, floppy ears sit low on the cocker's head. They may be so long that they fall in the dog's food dish! The cocker also has a **docked** tail.

Though small, cocker spaniels have endless energy.

CARE

Cocker spaniels fit in well with most families. They bond with children and may grow protective of them. These affectionate dogs enjoy human contact. Like any family member, they expect love and attention.

Cockers are gentle, loving, playful, and carefree. They like to run free in the country.

Cockers also enjoy city living as long as they get exercise.

These pets require regular grooming. Their long hair needs weekly or even daily brushing. This will keep their beautiful coats from becoming **matted** and tangled. Sometimes, the dogs need to be bathed and have their nails clipped.

To avoid irritating your cocker's skin, use a high-quality dog shampoo.

Like all dogs, cockers need **vaccines** for protection against diseases. Puppies should be **spayed** or **neutered**. A veterinarian can provide these services.

FEEDING

Dogs are carnivores, which means they enjoy meat. But they need to eat more than just meat. All dogs require a well-balanced diet. A high-quality commercial dog food will provide your cocker spaniel with the proper **nutrition**.

When you buy a puppy, continue feeding it the **breeder**'s diet. A small puppy needs four to five small meals a day. By six months, it will need only two meals daily. At about one year, a single feeding might be enough. However, many owners still prefer to feed their dogs twice a day.

Like any animal, a cocker needs a lot of fresh water. Water should be kept next to its food bowl and changed daily. Use sturdy bowls the dog can't tip over!

Proper nutrition is key to keeping a cocker happy and healthy.

THINGS THEY NEED

Every dog needs a quiet place to sleep. A soft dog bed in a quiet corner is perfect for an indoor cocker spaniel. If the dog lives outside, a dry doghouse will protect it from the weather. A fenced-in yard will also help keep your loving pet safe.

Cockers need exercise daily. Luckily, they love to walk and run. Playing together also keeps these dogs happy and healthy. And, toys will help keep them out of mischief when you are busy!

In most cities and towns, dogs must be leashed when going for a walk. In addition to a leash, owners need to purchase a collar and an identification tag.

This tag includes an owner's contact information. If his or her dog becomes lost, the owner can be called.

Playing with your cocker is a great way to bond.

PUPPIES

After mating, a female cocker spaniel is **pregnant** for about nine weeks. Her puppies are tiny and helpless when born. They rely on their mother for safety and food.

Do you think a cocker spaniel puppy is right for you? Be sure to find a reliable **breeder**. This will help make sure you get a healthy pet. Puppies can join new, loving families when they are eight weeks old.

A new puppy is a big responsibility! Training must begin right away. Let your puppy get used to its new home. Then, introduce it to new people and animals. This will help your dog grow into a lovable pet. A well cared for cocker will be a friendly family member for about 12 years.

Puppies cannot see or hear until 10 to 14 days after birth.

GLOSSARY

American Kennel Club - an organization that studies and promotes interest in purebred dogs.

breed - a group of animals sharing the same ancestors and appearance. A breeder is a person who raises animals. Raising animals is often called breeding them.

Canidae (KAN-uh-dee) - the scientific Latin name for the dog family. Members of this family are called canids. They include domestic dogs, wolves, jackals, foxes, and coyotes.

docked - cut short.

flush - to cause to fly or start up suddenly.

matted - formed into thick, tangled masses of hair.

muzzle - an animal's nose and jaws.

neuter (NOO-tuhr) - to remove a male animal's reproductive organs.

nutrition - that which provides energy and promotes growth, maintenance, and repair.

pregnant - having one or more babies growing within the body.

retrieve - to locate and bring in.

spay - to remove a female animal's reproductive organs.

vaccine (vak-SEEN) - a shot given to prevent illness or disease.

WEB SITES

To learn more about cocker spaniels, visit ABDO Publishing Company on the World Wide Web at **www.abdopublishing.com**. Web sites about cocker spaniels are featured on our Book Links page. These links are routinely monitored and updated to provide the most current information available.

INDEX